THE LITTLE
BOOK OF
confusables

Simple spelling and usage tips to help
smart people avoid stupid mistakes

Sarah Townsend

978-1-9163715-3-8
sarahtownsendeditorial.co.uk

Cover design: Lost & Found Creative
Page layout: Lost & Found Creative/George Townsend

Amy and George:

YOU'RE my inspiration. Without YOUR
PRESENCE, my life would contain a lot
LESS love (and FEWER PRESENTS).

PRAISE FOR THE
LITTLE BOOK OF CONFUSABLES

"I've been working with words for 20+ years and I still get plenty of these mixed up. Now, with this great little book on my desk, everything is clear!"

Tom Albrighton, Author, How to Write Clearly

"It's like a dictionary, but far more fun! Confused? Not anymore."

Vikki Ross, Copy Chief

"Incredibly useful for anyone who reads, writes or speaks. Beyond this book's utility, I love the fact that Sarah has produced an intensely nerdy book about language that manages to be a delight to read and a beauty to behold."

Leif Kendall, Director, ProCopywriters and CopyCon

*"Everyone needs **The Little Book of Confusables**! It's the gift that keeps on giving."*

Cat Roberts-Young, Copywriter, Cat Copy Creative

"Smart, witty, pithy, astute and informative. A great present for your line manager, who struggles with syntax and spelling."

Guy Horne, Managing Director, H&A Media

*"I always believed I was exceptional with words. However, if I hadn't checked with **The Little Book of Confusables**, that sentence could have looked very different. This book is a must, no matter how clever you think you are."*

Joelle Byrne, Business Strategist

"Aside from the horror of realising how very confused I've been for almost all my writing life, I have at last found something that will de-fuddle my brain. Bravo, yet again, Sarah for making something so very useful (and fun)!"

Andrew Boulton, Creative Advertising and Copywriting Lecturer

*"My team have benefited from Sarah's **confusables** posts for years. We write a lot of strategic documents and so we need to get things right. There's always that moment of 'is it **effect** or **affect**', '**principal** or **principle**'? This book is going to be essential!"*

**Louise King, Senior Planning Officer,
Gloucestershire Constabulary**

"We all have them. Those little words that make you stop in your tracks and think. Which is fine, until the flow of your words is **affected**... *or is it* **effected**?

The **effect** *of Sarah's new book is that you'll be able to find out – and fast. Which will* **affect** *the quality of your writing – and improve your confidence, too. (I promise not to ask which pages you turn down for quick reference, if you promise not to ask for mine...)"*

Katherine Wildman, Copywriter and Scriptwriter, Haydn Grey Copywriting Agency

"I've recommended Sarah's **confusables** *tips to delegates for years. To have them in one place – in such a gorgeously visual format – is just brilliant!"*

Emma Ewing, Director, Big Fish Training

"It's as if Sarah took my entire Google search history (err, the safe parts). And not only wrote down all the answers. But clever ways of remembering those answers, too. Giving me even more time to Google the other stuff."

Giles Edwards, Founder, Gasp!

"Every sub-editor should have a copy on their desk."

Rebecca Lowe, Poet, Journalist and Editor

"This book is amazing – no matter how many years you've been writing and no matter how much of a grammar nerd you are.

The Little Book of Confusables *will be one of those books you keep next to your computer at all times."*

Anna Gunning, Director, Gunning Marketing

*"Sarah certainly has a way with words! I've spent most of my life with the **affect**/**effect** conundrum, but no more thanks to this book. Sarah is your perfect guide. You're going to love it – as well as sharpen your writing skills."*

Mark Masters, Founder, You Are The Media

*"As someone who often gets confused between words like **bare** and **bear** it's great to see a book that explains everything so clearly. Plus it's absolutely gorgeous! I love the layout and the use of contrasting typefaces."*

Bhavini Lakhani, Graphic Designer and Branding Expert

INTRODUCTION

However confident you are as a writer – and however good your grasp of the English language – we all have blind spots.

Is it **LETS** or **LET'S**? **PRACTICE** or **PRACTISE**? **EFFECT** or **AFFECT**?

Using the wrong word can completely change your message – and lead to embarrassing mistakes!

- **BALD** men aren't always **BOLD**.

- **DISEASED** may be bad, but **DECEASED** is a whole lot worse.

- Dramatic **CORDS** require the fashion police.

- And heaven forbid you ask someone to '**BARE** with me' – unless you're a fan of getting naked with strangers.

I call these **confusables**, and I've been spotting and sharing them on social media since 2016.

Some of them have made it onto my website as popular blogs that help thousands of people each month improve their writing.

Other examples – many of which I've spotted out in the wild – have been added to my ever-growing collection of commonly confused words... which you're now holding in the palm of your hand.

The Little Book of Confusables is your guide to those tricky words even smart people screw up.

It contains simple, memorable spelling reminders and usage examples for almost 600 commonly confused words, to help you **boost your vocabulary**, **write with confidence** and **avoid embarrassing mistakes**.

WHAT'S INCLUDED?

The Little Book of Confusables contains:

- Spelling tips and usage examples for hundreds of commonly confused words – from **THERE, THEIR + THEY'RE, ACUTE + CHRONIC, LETS + LET'S** and **COMPLIMENT + COMPLEMENT** to **LEND + BORROW, PARAMETER + PERIMETER, LESS + FEWER** and **POISONOUS + VENOMOUS**.

- Handy hints to avoid mistakes like **DOGGY DOG WORLD**, **DAMP SQUID**, **OFF YOUR OWN BACK** and **OLD WISE TALE**.

- The difference between **HOMOPHONES**, **HOMONYMS**, **HOMOGRAPHS**, **EGGCORNS** and **MALAPROPISMS**.

... all in this gorgeous, flickable, fits-in-your-bag format.

WHY I WROTE THIS BOOK

I've been a copywriter and editor for almost 30 years, using words to help businesses get results from their marketing. I also wrote the bestselling – and super straight-talking – guide to self-employment, **Survival Skills for Freelancers**, which has helped entrepreneurs in more than 20 countries grow in confidence and find freelance success.

I believe clear, human language is one of the most powerful tools we have – but it doesn't come easy to all of us. Over the years, I've worked with thousands of smart people who find English less than intuitive. (I feel the same about maths!) And even the writers, editors and proofreaders among us have to look stuff up.

While some people choose to be outraged by 'shocking falling standards of English', I prefer to see mistakes as an opportunity for learning.

On the basis that we learn best when we're having fun, **The Little Book of Confusables** is designed to amuse, entertain and inform.

It's a book that'll feed your love of language. A book you'll want to keep close at all times. A book that'll stop you tripping up and looking daft.

I'm less concerned with identifying word types throughout, and more focused on helping you to remember the difference. That said, I've included a summary of **confusables** categories on the following page.

As Leif Kendall, Director of ProCopywriters, said: "I love the fact that Sarah has produced an intensely nerdy book about language that manages to be a delight to read and a beauty to behold." I hope you enjoy it.

Sarah Townsend
Author

CONFUSABLES CATEGORIES

Homophones: words that sound the same but have different meanings.

Homographs: words that are spelled the same but have different meanings.

Homonyms: which can be homographs, homophones or both.

Malapropisms: which occur when a similar-sounding wrong word is used instead of the right word, with nonsensical and often funny results.

Eggcorns: which occur when a word in a phrase is replaced by a similar-sounding word that arguably makes sense – like **OLD WISE TALE**.

Miscellaneous: random oddities, such as **ASSUME + PRESUME**, **LIBEL + SLANDER** and **OBJECTIVE + SUBJECTIVE**.

HOW TO USE THIS BOOK

The words in this book are shared in alphabetical order: **AFFECT + EFFECT**, for example, is listed under A, not E. As a result, some letters are missing from **The Little Book of Confusables**. While I'd have liked every letter to feature, my priority was usability.

Word class (noun, verb, etc) generally only appears next to words that have a different meaning when the word class is altered. In the example above, **EFFECT** is a noun, but it can also – more rarely – be a verb. (I made an exception where I felt adding the word class helped with understanding. My book, my rules, right?!)

Some words have many different definitions and including them all would've made this an incredibly long book! For the sake of simplicity, I've included the most common definitions, as these tend to be the ones that are most often confused.

Finally, my tips and examples are based on British English usage. While I hope **The Little Book of Confusables** reaches and helps English speakers around the world, some content may not apply to all audiences.

a

accept

Acknowledge or agree to receive.

except

Apart from or excluding.

REMEMBER

The AC of ACCEPT and ACknowledge.

The EX of EXCEPT and EXcluding.

EXAMPLE

"I ACCEPT that there are EXCEPTIONS to this rule."

---

accepted

Acknowledged or agreed to receive.

excepted

Excluded or left out.

REMEMBER

The AC of ACCEPTED and ACknowledged.

The EX of EXCEPTED and EXcluded.

EXAMPLE

"I'm not a fan of lawyers. Present company EXCEPTED!"

"Rude! Apology ACCEPTED, I guess."

When referring to illness...

acute

means sudden and severe, while...

chronic

means worsening over time.

REMEMBER

To remember CHRONIC, it helps to know that the prefix CHRON means **time** (as in CHRONological and anaCHRONistic).

adapt

Change to become used to something new.

adept

Skilled or technically proficient.

adopt

Choose to take up something.

EXAMPLE

"I've ADEPTLY ADAPTED to the cat I've ADOPTED."

---

adverse

Harmful or unfavourable. Often used with **effects** or **conditions**.

averse

Having a strong dislike for something. Usually used with **to**.

EXAMPLE

"I'm not AVERSE to taking medication – but I'll stop if I develop any ADVERSE side-effects."

advice (noun)

Suggestions or encouragement.

advise (verb)

Suggest or encourage.

REMEMBER

As with PRACTICE and PRACTISE, remember
that ICE is the noun. That's good ADVICE.

EXAMPLE

"I would ADVISE you to take ADVICE on the matter."

---

affect (verb)

Alter or influence.

effect (noun)

End result.

REMEMBER

A for AFFECT and Alter. E for EFFECT and End result.

EXAMPLE

"The short winter days AFFECT my mood."

"Really? What's the EFFECT?"

"I feel lethargic and sad."

aggravated

Irritated, or made worse (often in relation to a crime).

agitated

Nervous, troubled or unsettled.

REMEMBER

Think of VATED in AGGRAVATED and eleVATED.

An AGGRAVATED crime leads to an eleVATED sentence.

EXAMPLE

"The jury picked up on his AGITATED demeanour
and found him guilty of AGGRAVATED assault."

aid

Help or assistance.

aide

An assistant to an important person.

REMEMBER

AIDE is a far less common word than AID, and only has one meaning. For any other meaning, use AID.

EXAMPLE

"The AIDE provided AID to Ade."

ail

Feel unwell, or make physically or mentally ill.

ale

A type of beer.

REMEMBER

Amber-coloured beer is called pALE ALE.

EXAMPLE

"What AILS you?"

"Not sure. Perhaps I had too much ALE last night!"

aisle

A path between two columns or rows, usually found in a supermarket or church.

isle

A small island.

i'll

A contraction of **I will** or **I shall**.

a lot

A large quantity.

allot

Give a share of something for a particular purpose.

REMEMBER

ALLOTments are divided into shares. Both words are commonly misspelled as ALOT, which is not a word.

EXAMPLE

"A LOT of people struggle to ALLOT their time well."

---

allowed

Permitted.

aloud

Audibly or out loud.

REMEMBER

ALOUD ends with LOUD. ALLOWED starts with ALLOW, which means **permit**.

EXAMPLE

"You know you're not ALLOWED to talk ALOUD?"

allude

Refer to something indirectly.

elude

Escape or avoid.

REMEMBER

ELUDE and Escape both start with E.

EXAMPLE

"You ALLUDE that I ELUDE the law?
Are you trying to get me arrested?!"

---

allusion

Indirect reference.

elusion

Escaping or avoiding.

illusion

Deceptive appearance.

EXAMPLE

"Your ALLUSION to my ELUSION of the law was mere ILLUSION? In that case, I forgive you."

altar

A table or raised area where a religious ritual occurs.

alter

Change or modify something.

REMEMBER

ALTAR contains the TA of TAble. An ALTER ego is a
secret identity (think Peter Parker and Spider-Man).
An ALTAR ego is not a thing.

EXAMPLE

"Please ALTER the position of the flowers on the ALTAR."

---

amount

Used for things you **can't** count: information, rain, coffee. These are called mass nouns.

number

Used for things you **can** count: facts, rainy days, cups of coffee. These are called count nouns.

REMEMBER

If you want to NUMBER a group of things, you need to be able to count them first.

antipathy

A deep-seated and intense dislike or hostility.

apathy

A lack of interest or concern.

REMEMBER

The prefix ANTI in ANTIPATHY means **against**
(as in disliking) and the prefix A in APATHY means
without (as in without interest). Or just picture
a bored, APATHETIC APe. Works for me!

---

any way

Any one out of all possible ways.

anyway

Regardless. Often used to change a subject or end

a conversation. ANYWAY...

REMEMBER

Only use ANYWAY if it can be replaced with ANYhow.

(Both are one word in this context.)

EXAMPLE

"ANYWAY, let me know if I can help in ANY WAY."

ascent

Climb or upward movement.

assent

Approval.

REMEMBER

Climb starts with C, which is found in ASCENT.

EXAMPLE

"Houston ASSENTED to our ASCENT!

Let's go to the moon!"

aspirational

Intended to encourage a desire for status

or upward social mobility.

inspirational

Intended to inspire.

REMEMBER

Think of the root words, ASPIRE and INSPIRE.

Those quotes you see online are INSPIRATIONAL,

while glossy magazines containing full-page photos of

beautiful homes and luxury lifestyles are ASPIRATIONAL.

assistance

Help.

assistant

The person providing the help.

assistants

More than one ASSISTANT. Obviously.

EXAMPLE

"As my new ASSISTANT, you'll provide ASSISTANCE with my daily tasks, like my previous ASSISTANTS."

---

assume

Think something without proof or evidence.

presume

Think something based on probability.

REMEMBER

The PR of PRESUME and PRobability, or the well-known phrase 'when you ASSUME, you make an ASS of U and ME'.

EXAMPLE

"How dare you ASSUME I ate all the cake? I PRESUME you have evidence to back up your accusation?"

bail

Leave a place or situation, or the payment required to temporarily free someone accused of a crime.

bale

A large wad of material, such as hay or straw.

REMEMBER

You pay someone's BAIL to get them out of jAIL.

EXAMPLE

"These hay BALES are too heavy! I'm gonna BAIL."

baited

Taunted, deliberately annoyed or enticed.

bated

A Shakespearean shortening of abated,
meaning decreased or reduced.

REMEMBER

BAITED is the more common word. BATED is rarely used
outside the expression 'with BATED breath' – first used
in The Merchant of Venice in 1605 – which means
'with nervous excitement'.

bald

Hairless.

bold

Brave.

REMEMBER

Think of knights of OLD, who were always BOLD.

A BALD man isn't always a BOLD man – though

Dwayne Johnson and Vin Diesel's movie roles

may have you believing otherwise.

balmy

Pleasantly warm.

barmy

An informal word for crazy.

REMEMBER

The L in BALMY and Lovely weather.

The R in BARMY and cRazy.

EXAMPLE

"Spring weather is often BALMY but you'd have
to be BARMY to sunbathe that early in the year!"

bare

Exposed, or the act of exposing.

bear

Endure, carry, or a large furry animal.

REMEMBER

BARE always means exposed or naked – think of it as
Belly, Abs and Rear End! Need someone to be patient?
Ask them to 'BEAR with me' not 'BARE with me'.
(This is one you **really** don't want to get wrong!)

base (noun)

A foundation, or the bottom of something.

base (verb)

Locate.

bass

Low pitched, as a voice or an instrument.

EXAMPLE

"I'm BASED in the BASS section of the choir.

We BASE our performances on show tunes."

baseline

The starting point in a comparison.

bassline

The lowest line in a piece of music.

REMEMBER

Your BASELINE is unlikely to be funky. Unless you've been dabbling in some creative accounting, I guess...

EXAMPLE

"The funky James Brown hit was the BASELINE for my BASSLINE."

bazaar

A market in a Middle Eastern country, or a charity event.

bizarre

Strange, peculiar or weird.

REMEMBER

Something BIZARRE is Really Really Eccentric.

EXAMPLE

"Your Christmas BAZAAR may be BIZARRE,

but it's nothing compared to ours!"

---

beach (noun)

A sandy or pebbled area on the coast.

beach (verb)

Pull something out of the water and up onto the BEACH.

beech

A large tree with pale bark, popular with squirrels.

REMEMBER

The EE in both BEECH and trEE and the EA in both BEACH and sEA.

beat (noun)

Rhythm in a piece of music.

beat (verb)

Defeat, strike or whisk.

beet

Shortening of beetroot: a hard, purple root vegetable.

EXAMPLE

"I BEAT my BEET to the BEAT of Michael Jackson's
BEAT It. I looked a bit weird but I didn't care."

---

beside

Next to or alongside.

besides

Apart from or as well as.

REMEMBER

Think of the two Ss in aS well aS to remember
that BESIDES has two Ss.

EXAMPLE

"I sat BESIDE Kamal at the networking dinner today."

"Oh really? Who else was there BESIDES Kamal?"

---

board (noun)

A thin piece of flat wood, or a group of decision makers.

board (verb)

Enter a plane or train.

bored

Uninterested, or lacking challenge.

EXAMPLE

"Don't get caught looking BORED in the BOARD meeting. The CEO won't let you BOARD his private jet!"

---

borrow

Take something from someone with the understanding that you'll return it after use.

lend

Give something to someone with the understanding that they'll return it after use.

REMEMBER

LEND is connected to **give**. BORROW is connected to **take**.

EXAMPLE

"I need to BORROW a car – can you LEND me yours?"

---

bought

Past tense of buy.

brought

Past tense of bring.

REMEMBER

The BR in BRing and BROUGHT.

EXAMPLE

"You like my sombrero? I BOUGHT it in Spain and BROUGHT it home on the plane."

brake

Stopping pedal (or use of the stopping pedal).

break (noun)

Time out.

break (verb)

Damage or destroy.

REMEMBER

Cars BRAKE. Plates BREAK. You take a lunch BREAK.

You might use your BRAKES to make sure nothing BREAKS.

---

bread

Staple foodstuff.

bred

Born and raised.

REMEMBER

The common expression is 'born and BRED'
not 'born and BREAD'.

EXAMPLE

"He was born and BRED in Shaftesbury,
where the famous ad for BREAD was filmed."

---

breadth

Another word for width, or the extent of something.

breath

A full cycle of breathing.

breathe

Inhale and exhale.

REMEMBER

Imagine breathing in to the long EEEEE sound in the word BREATHE to remember it ends in E. "And BREATHE…"

bridal

Relating to a bride or wedding.

bridle

Headgear used to control a horse.

REMEMBER

Unless you work in the equestrian industry, you're unlikely to need the spelling BRIDLE. A pre-wedding gathering is known as a BRIDAL shower. I, for one, don't fancy getting caught in a BRIDLE shower. Ouch!

broach

Initiate a topic of conversation.

brooch

A decorative pin.

REMEMBER

To remember the A in BROACH, think of how bringing up a difficult topic of conversation can be Awkward. To remember the OO in BROOCH, think of two round pin badges stuck to a jacket.

bud

Part of a plant that will develop into a leaf or flower, or an informal term for a friend.

butt (noun)

Target, the end of something, or buttocks.

butt (verb)

Knock against. Often used with **heads**.

EXAMPLE

"Nip it in the BUD, not BUTT! That's harassment, BUD."

---

buy

Make a purchase, or believe something you're told.

by

A preposition meaning next to.

bye

Synonym of ciao, later alligator and more.

EXAMPLE

"Before you say BYE, come BY and BUY more from us!"

C

callous

Hard or unfeeling.

callus

Localised thickening of the skin.

call us

Instructions on a takeaway menu.

REMEMBER

The OU in CALLOUS, and how a CALLOUS
remark might make you go "Ooo, OUch!".

cannon

Large mounted weapon.

canon

Most commonly an established principle or rule,
or the complete works of a famous writer.

REMEMBER

Picture the CANNON mounted between the two Ns.

EXAMPLE

"The CANON of Sherlock Holmes consists of four novels
and 56 short stories written by Sir Arthur Conan Doyle."

canva

Graphic design program.

canvas

Strong cloth used to make tents and sails.

canvass

Solicit votes.

EXAMPLE

"The councillor distributed CANVA leaflets from his CANVAS bag to CANVASS votes."

---

card sharp

Someone who makes money by cheating at card games.

card shark

Someone who makes money by cheating at card games.

REMEMBER

CARD SHARP is the more common expression in British English and CARD SHARK is more common in American English, where it also refers to a skilled card player. To remember the difference, think of how few SHARKs are found in Britain.

---

caught

Past tense of catch.

court

Place where ball games are played,
or legal decisions are made.

REMEMBER

Both CAUGHT and CAtch start with CA.

EXAMPLE

"CAUGHT criminals are taken to COURT."

cedilla

Wiggly little hook below the letter C in some languages, like this: ç.

quesadilla

A Mexican dish, consisting of two tortillas stuffed with cheese and other yumminess.

REMEMBER

Think of how cheese (QUESo in Spanish) blends with the tortILLA to make the QUESADILLA. And don't confuse the two. Diacritics taste rubbish.

chest of drawers

Unit in your bedroom where you keep your socks. Not...

chester drawers

Unless you bought your drawers from CHESTER,

in which case, I won't argue with you.

REMEMBER

A CHEST is an item of furniture, so this should be

an easy one to remember. (For the record, it's not

a CHEST OF DRAWS or a CHESTER DRAWS, either.)

choose

Select.

chose

Past tense of CHOOSE.

REMEMBER

CHOOSE – which is present tense – rhymes with news, which, by definition, happens in the present.

EXAMPLE

"Last week I CHOSE to CHOOSE my words wisely. This week, I got into trouble for speaking my mind."

---

chords

A group of musical notes sounded together.

cords

Short for corduroy trousers – an item of clothing, popular in the 1970s – or a synonym for cables.

REMEMBER

The H of Hear and CHORDS. You can Hear CHORDS.

EXAMPLE

"Dramatic CHORDS create suspense.
Dramatic CORDS require the fashion police."

cite

Reference a source of information to reinforce a point.

sight

The ability to see.

site

A place, or the shortened version of website.

EXAMPLE

"I CITED this SITE in my essay but, with my poor SIGHT, I misspelled the URL. Oops!"

---

coherent

Consistent and fitting together as an idea.

cohesive

Sticking together, or unified.

REMEMBER

The SIVE of COHESIVE and adheSIVE (a synonym for glue)
– both of which relate to sticking together.

EXAMPLE

"Our plan is COHERENT and our team is COHESIVE.
This can't go wrong."

---

collaborate

Work together towards a shared goal.

cooperate

Help someone out.

corroborate

Provide evidence to support something.

EXAMPLE

"They COOPERATED with the police to CORROBORATE the case against the two COLLABORATING suspects."

---

compare

Examine the differences or similarities between two or more things.

compere

Event host.

REMEMBER

"'Ello ladeez and gentlemen, it's your COMPERE 'ERE."

EXAMPLE

"Best not to COMPARE the COMPERE to the star performer. They might take offence."

---

complement

Match or complete.

compliment

Praise or a flattering remark.

REMEMBER

The two Es in complEtE and COMPLEMENT.

Think eye (i) in the COMPLIMENT 'you have beautiful eyes'.

EXAMPLE

"That top COMPLEMENTS your skin tone."

"What a nice COMPLIMENT – thanks!"

complementary

Completing or enhancing something else.

complimentary

Free, or a flattering remark.

REMEMBER

The two Es in complEtE and COMPLEMENTARY.

EXAMPLE

"That COMPLIMENTARY olive bread COMPLEMENTED the soup perfectly. My COMPLIMENTS to the chef!"

confidant

Someone you confide in. Also, confidante (female).

confident

Sure of yourself.

REMEMBER

Picture whispering your secrets to a friendly ANT
– your tiny CONFIDANT. If you're CONFIDENT,
your ego is less likely to DENT.

EXAMPLE

"Are you CONFIDENT you can trust your CONFIDANT?"

conscience

An inner feeling of right and wrong.

conscious

Awake or aware.

REMEMBER

If you're passed out, you're unCONSCIOUS.

There's no such word as unCONSCIENCE.

EXAMPLE

"I'm very CONSCIOUS that guy is acting
like he has a guilty CONSCIENCE."

---

consequently

As a result.

subsequently

Next in a sequence.

REMEMBER

Think of the connection between CONSEQUENTLY
and CONSEQUENCE – the result or effect of an action.
Imagine the CONSEQUENCES of getting these words
mixed up – and the SUBSEQUENT embarrassment.

---

constant

Happening all the time. Unchanging.

continual

Starting and stopping frequently.

continuous

Occurring without interruption. Never stopping.

EXAMPLE

"Their CONTINUAL arguing is driving me crazy..."

"Just be grateful it's not CONTINUOUS!"

When referring to illness...

contagious

means spread through direct contact, while...

infectious

means spread by an agent such as bacteria.

REMEMBER

Think of the CONT in CONTAGIOUS and CONTact.

All CONTAGIOUS diseases are INFECTIOUS
– such as the common cold. But not all INFECTIOUS
diseases are CONTAGIOUS – such as food poisoning.

contiguous

Sharing a boundary or edge. Abutting or touching.

continuous

Occurring without interruption. Never stopping.

REMEMBER

The root word CONTINUE in CONTINUOUS.

The playground game where someone is touched to be tagged 'it' – often called TIG – in CONTIGUOUS.

coo

Speak in a gentle voice, or the sound a dove makes.

coup

A major achievement – often unexpected – or a sudden, violent taking of government power. (The P is silent).

coop

Hen house.

REMEMBER

If you're confined in a small space, you're 'COOPED up'.

could of

This is a mishearing of...

could've

A contraction of **could have**.

REMEMBER

Think of the VE of haVE and COULD'VE.

And never write COULD OF – it's always wrong.

The same goes for WOULD OF and SHOULD OF.

EXAMPLE

"You COULD'VE gone with her if you'd known!"

---

counsellor

A therapist or advisor. Someone who helps you unpack your emotional issues.

councillor

A local government officer.

REMEMBER

A COUNSELLOR is paid to advise. They SELL their time. Think of the SELL in COUNSELLOR. To remember COUNCILLOR, think of the spelling of local COUNCIL.

---

counterfeit

Fake. Often used with **goods**. Not...

counterfit

Little-known American rock band. Or...

counter-fit

Install a new kitchen, perhaps?

REMEMBER

The silent E in COUNTERFEIT means it's pronounced the same as COUNTERFIT and COUNTER-FIT.

cue

Something that signals the right time for something else to happen. Important for actors.

queue

A line of people waiting, or the act of waiting in a QUEUE.

REMEMBER

QUEUE is a longer word – and we can all relate to waiting a long time in a QUEUE. Or think of the letters UEUE QUEUING up behind the Q. Something that happens bang on time is 'right on CUE'.

cumulated

Gathered or amassed.

cumulative

Increased in size thanks to consecutive additions.
Often used with **effect**.

REMEMBER

Eating one chocolate bar won't have an adverse effect,
but the CUMULATIVE effect of eating multiple chocolate
bars each day could be weight gain. CUMULATED
is a verb, synonymous with ACCUMULATED.

curb

Limit or restrain. Also the American English spelling of the British English word, KERB.

kerb

The raised edge of a pavement or path.

REMEMBER

The American sitcom is 'CURB Your Enthusiasm'.

EXAMPLE

"You need to CURB your spending habits."

"Parking on the KERB is bad for your tyres."

cypress

Fir tree.

cyprus

Island in the Mediterranean Sea.

REMEMBER

Think of a family holiday in the sun to remember 'the photo of US in CYPRUS'.

EXAMPLE

"Do CYPRESS trees grow in CYPRUS?"

d

damp squib

An event or situation that's disappointing because
it's much less impressive than expected. Not...

damp squid

SQUID live in the sea. They're already pretty wet.

REMEMBER

A SQUIB is a type of firework. A DAMP SQUIB is one
that fizzles out and doesn't explode. So disappointing...

deceased

No longer living.

diseased

Unwell.

REMEMBER

These are two words you **really** don't want to get mixed up! To help you remember the difference, think of DISEASED as being affected by a DISEASE, while DECEASED literally means 'CEASED to exist'.

decent

Appropriate or satisfactory.

descent

Drop or downward movement.

dissent

Disagreement.

EXAMPLE

"The pilot DISSENTED to the request for
DESCENT until the weather was DECENT."

---

dependant

A person who depends on you, such as your child.

dependent

Reliant upon.

REMEMBER

Think of a DEPENDANT aunty ANT. In my head she has a lace bonnet and a basket of flowers. The clearer the picture, the better it works.

EXAMPLE

"Your DEPENDANTS are DEPENDENT on you."

---

desert (noun)

Sandy region.

desert (verb)

Abandon.

dessert

Pudding.

REMEMBER

Think of the SS as a double helping of DESSERT. And don't get DESERT in your DESSERT, or you'll have to DESERT it!

---

device (noun)

A contraption or piece of electronic equipment.

devise (verb)

Create.

REMEMBER

The endings of these two follow the same rule
as PRACTICE and PRACTISE. ICE is the noun.

EXAMPLE

"I DEVISED a plan for using the DEVICE."

dinghy

Small boat.

dingy

Dull.

REMEMBER

These two may look similar but they're pronounced differently. Remember that DINGY rhymes with stINGY.

EXAMPLE

"A DINGY day is not the time for a DINGHY ride."

---

disc

A thin, flat, circular object.

disk

A storage device used in computing.

REMEMBER

In British English, DISC describes a thin, flat, circular object – such as a compact DISC – while DISK is more common in computer-related use, such as a hard DISK. To remember the difference, think of the C of Circular.

---

discreet

Tactful or careful in actions and speech.

discrete

Individual or separate.

REMEMBER

DISCRETE contains CRETE – an island that's individual or separate from mainland Greece. You might have a range of 'DISCRETE skills', not 'DISCREET skills'. (Unless you're great at keeping secrets, of course.)

disinterested

Impartial or not biased.

uninterested

Not interested.

REMEMBER

No wonder there's so much confusion around these two: the original definition of UNINTERESTED was **not biased** while DISINTERESTED meant **not interested**! Today, synonyms of UNINTERESTED include UNmoved, UNcaring, UNfeeling, UNenthusiastic. All the UNs: except UNbiased!

distinct

Separate, or clearly different from another thing.

distinctive

A prominent identifying feature.

REMEMBER

Think about the IVE in DISTINCTIVE. You might
say 'I'VE got DISTINCTIVE green eyes' (lucky you).

EXAMPLE

"The DISTINCTIVE red breast of the robin makes
it clearly DISTINCT from other small birds."

dog-eat-dog

The phrase 'DOG-EAT-DOG world' means brutal, ruthless and competitive. It's commonly misheard as...

doggy dog

Alas, 'DOGGY DOG world' is not a thing – but if a canine brand hasn't seized the idea for their annual expo...

REMEMBER

Think of two DOGS, teeth bared, ready to EAT.

EXAMPLE

"Up your game. It's a DOG-EAT-DOG world out there!"

donator

Someone who donates. Though technically correct,
this word is far less common than...

donor

which also means someone who donates.

REMEMBER

If in doubt, choose the simpler word.

EXAMPLE

"I DONATE blood regularly. That makes me a DONOR.
And a lifesaver!"

draft

A rough document.

draught

Cool air, or beer served from a barrel (not a bottle).

REMEMBER

The popular board game – known in American
English as checkers – is spelled DRAUGHTS.

EXAMPLE

"Don't spill your DRAUGHT on your DRAFT while
working in a DRAUGHT (or ever, preferably)."

draw

Make an image on paper, or take out
(often refers to cash or a weapon).

drawer

Someone who draws. Or where your keep your DRAWERS.

drawers

Informal term for knickers. Or more than one DRAWER.

EXAMPLE

"I left the DRAWING of my DRAWERS in my DRAWER."

---

e

eclipse

When one celestial body blocks the light from another.

ellipse

A two-dimensional shape, similar to an oval.

ellipses

The plural of ELLIPSE and ELLIPSIS.

ellipsis

A series of three dots used to build suspense or indicate that a word or phrase is missing from a sentence.

elder (noun)

A small tree, known for its edible flowers and berries.

elder (adjective)

The opposite of younger.

older

Also the opposite of younger.

REMEMBER

OLDER and ELDER are often used interchangeably, but
ELDER only describes people. OLDER also describes things.

elicit

Draw out.

illicit

Illegal or wrong.

REMEMBER

ILLICIT and ILLegal both start with ILL.

EXAMPLE

"I tried my best to ELICIT stories of his ILLICIT activity but he was having none of it."

---

emaciated

Thin and frail because of a lack of nutrition.

emancipated

Freed.

emasculated

Threatened someone's masculinity.

REMEMBER

Think of the similarity between EMASCULATE
and MASCULine. A freed MAN is EMANCIPATED.

---

emigrate

Leave your country to live in another.

immigrate

Come to another country to live.

REMEMBER

EMIGRATE refers to **leaving**, while IMMIGRATE refers to **arrival**. Think E for EMIGRATE and Exit.

EXAMPLE

"My grandpa EMIGRATED from Ireland in the 1920s and IMMIGRATED to America to find work."

emit

Discharge, secrete or emanate.

omit

Leave out, or fail to include.

REMEMBER

The EM of EMIT and EManate, and the O of Out and OMIT.

EXAMPLE

"You OMIT to mention in your message that the machine EMITS a strange smell."

enervate

Weaken. The opposite of INNERVATE.

innervate

Supply part of the body with nerves.

innovate

Introduce new ideas.

REMEMBER

INNERVATE is sometimes used figuratively, to mean 'stimulate to action'. Think INNERVATE and NERVes.

entomology

The study of insects.

etymology

The study of the origins of words and their meanings.

REMEMBER

ENTOMOLOGY sounds a little like it starts with the word ANT, which is an insect. Tenuous, but it works.

EXAMPLE

"What's the ETYMOLOGY of the word ENTOMOLOGY?"

every day

Exactly as it sounds – happening each day.

everyday

Commonplace or regular.

REMEMBER

If you can replace EVERY with each, it's two words.

EXAMPLE

"Seeing EVERYDAY and EVERY DAY confused is an EVERYDAY occurrence."

exacerbate

Make something worse.

exasperate

Infuriate.

REMEMBER

EXASPERATE and iRATE share the same ending.

EXAMPLE

"You EXASPERATE me with your constant nagging.
It just EXACERBATES the situation!"

exciting

Causing eagerness or excitement.

exiting

In the process of leaving an area.

EXAMPLE

'Give way to EXITING vehicles' is a common road sign, indicating the right of way of vehicles leaving an area. I once spotted a sign saying 'Give way to EXCITING vehicles'. I assume it was a typo. Otherwise I'm thinking carnival floats, ice cream vans, the Batmobile...

f

faint

Feelings of weakness or dizziness.

Also feeble, or barely noticeable.

feint

A sneaky move. With **ruled**, lined writing paper.

REMEMBER

FAINT is by far the more common word. Something scary can be described as 'not for the FAINT-hearted', you might 'leave a FAINT trace', while being 'damned with FAINT praise' is to be given a backhanded compliment.

fair

Reasonable and just, or a fairground or event.

fare

Price paid to travel.

fayre

An archaic spelling of FAIR, sometimes used
to give something an olde-worlde vibe.

EXAMPLE

"The return FARE to the Christmas FAYRE was FAIR."

fate

Destiny, or a power that predetermines events.

fête

A celebration or public event, often for charity.

REMEMBER

The circumflex above the first E of FÊTE is a bit
like a party hat – and a FÊTE is a bit like a party.

EXAMPLE

"They met at the village FÊTE. She says it was FATE."

father

Male parent.

farther

More distant, physically.

further

More distant, figuratively.

REMEMBER

'How FAR?' is linked to 'How much FARTHER?'.

A restaurant might be closed 'until FURTHER notice'.

---

faze

Disturb.

phase

A period of time, or stage.

phaser

Weapon used on Star Trek, or a sound-altering device.

EXAMPLE

"My daughter is going through a tricky PHASE but
I won't let it FAZE me."

---

feasible

Possible or likely to succeed as an action.

plausible

Possible or likely to be true as a statement.

REMEMBER

To remember FEASIBLE think of a possible FEAt
(another word for an action). For PLAUSIBLE,
imagine a PLAUSIBLE statement generating a
round of apPLAUSe, or remember that Proclamation
– a synonym for statement – also begins with P.

fewer

Used for things you **can** count: words, buttons, cupcakes. These are called count nouns.

less

Used for things you **can't** count: sunshine, work, coffee. These are called mass nouns.

EXAMPLE

"I asked for FEWER hours at work so I could spend LESS of my time in the office."

finally

Eventually, or at last.

finely

Delicately. Often used with **chopped**.

REMEMBER

FINE means small or thin. If you cut something
FINELY you'll end up with FINE pieces.

EXAMPLE

"Once you've FINELY chopped that carrot I can
FINALLY get this soup on the go."

---

flammable

Easily set on fire.

inflammable

Easily set on fire. Oh.

REMEMBER

These two look like opposites but are virtually synonymous. Strictly speaking, something that's INFLAMMABLE is highly combustible, while something FLAMMABLE is simply capable of being set on fire. FLAMMABLE is the simpler and more common word.

flaunt

Show off.

flout

Disregard or ignore.

REMEMBER

To remember FLAUNT, imagine an AUNT
who is known for being a huge show off.

EXAMPLE

"The students FLOUTED the school's rules on
uniform and FLAUNTED their brightest clothes."

flounder (noun)

A flat fish.

flounder (verb)

Struggle mentally, or move with difficulty.

founder

Someone who establishes something.

EXAMPLE

"The FLOUNDER was the proud FOUNDER
of this school of fish."

foreword

A short introduction at the start of a book, written by someone other than the author.

forward

In the ahead direction.

REMEMBER

A FOREWORD consists of many WORDS (not wards).

EXAMPLE

"If you read FORWARDS, you'll find the FOREWORD after the title page."

---

formally

In accordance with etiquette or convention.

formerly

In the past, or before.

REMEMBER

The root of the word FORMERLY is FORMER.

EXAMPLE

"I was FORMERLY known as Sarah Saunders.
Now I'm FORMALLY known as Ms Townsend."

fortuitous

A chance result or event.

fortunate

Lucky.

REMEMBER

These two are often used interchangeably, and the difference in meanings continues to blur. Though the original definition of FORTUITOUS had no implication of luck or positivity, some thesauruses today list FORTUNATE as a synonym of FORTUITOUS.

freeze

Stop moving, or turn to ice.

frieze

A painted or sculpted band of decoration on a building.

REMEMBER

FREEZE is by far the more common spelling.

Tourists might visit Athens to view the famous

Parthenon FRIEZE. Think of the IE in vIEw and FRIEZE.

EXAMPLE

"FREEZE! Hands off the ancient FRIEZE!"

gaff

British slang for home, or a fishing spear.

gaffe

A mistake, faux pas or embarrassing error.

REMEMBER

The E of Embarrassing Error is present – albeit silent
– in GAFFE. The colloquial phrase 'blow the GAFF'
means to reveal a secret – especially in a public way.

gauge (noun)

A tool or measuring device, often used with **fuel**.

gauge (verb)

Assess or measure.

gouge

Cut, scoop or force something out.

REMEMBER

The A in GAUGE and Assess. There's no such word as GUAGE (so why do I type it every time I mean GAUGE?!).

---

gesture

An intentional movement – such as a nod or pointed finger – intended to convey a meaning.

jester

A historical clown hired to entertain royalty.

REMEMBER

Think of the J of Joke and JESTER. While 'a JESTER of goodwill' sounds like someone we'd all like to meet, an act of service carried out for someone else is 'a GESTURE of goodwill'.

Someone who goes all out to achieve success is a...

go-getter

Not a...

goal-getter

REMEMBER

Who knows? Language is a living, breathing thing. Perhaps one day GO-GETTER will evolve into the entirely logical-sounding GOAL-GETTER. For the time being, GOAL-GETTER is a mishearing of GO-GETTER.

gorilla

The largest of the great apes.

guerrilla

Someone who engages in irregular warfare.

REMEMBER

GUERRILLA has its roots in GUERRA: Spanish for war.

Sometimes spelled GUERILLA, it can also be used

to describe actions devised to take you by surprise.

The phrase 'GUERRILLA marketing' was created

in the 1980s by Jay Conrad Levinson.

grate (verb)

Annoy, or shred – usually food – into small pieces.

grate (noun)

Metal bars covering an opening.

great

One step down from amazing. One step up from good.

REMEMBER

You GRATED the cheese, they ATE the cheese.

Got that? GREAT!

guillemet

One of a pair of punctuation marks (« »)
used as speech marks in French.

guillemot

A sea bird that nests on cliff edges.

REMEMBER

These two look super similar but are pronounced
very differently. While GUILLEMOT is spoken as
it looks, GUILLEMET is pronounced ghi-may.

hair

Covers your head. Usually.

hare

Long-eared animal, like a rabbit but larger.

heir

A person due to inherit on the death of another person.

EXAMPLE

"He is the sole HEIR to his family's fortune, which consists of a taxidermy HARE and a ton of HAIRspray."

---

hear

The act of listening to something.

here

In this place.

REMEMBER

You use your EAR to HEAR. If you agree with something and want to show your approval, the expression is spelled 'HEAR, HEAR', not 'HERE, HERE'.

EXAMPLE

"Turn that down! I can't HEAR myself think in HERE!"

heard

Listened to, or been told about.

herd (noun)

A large group of animals.

herd (verb)

Control the movement of a crowd.

EXAMPLE

"I HEARD that farmers are skilled HERD HERDERS."

he's

A contraction of **he is** or **he has**.

his

Belonging to him.

REMEMBER

If you can replace the word with **he is** or **he has**, always write HE'S.

EXAMPLE

"HE'S gone to the pub" is right.

"HIS gone to the pub" is wrong.

historic

Important or significant in history.

historical

Something that happened in the past.

REMEMBER

A Jane Austen novel or an old map are HISTORICAL.
The site of an important battle, England's 1966 World
Cup win or the Magna Carta are HISTORIC. Any day that
happened in the past can be described as 'a HISTORICAL
day', while only the most significant are HISTORIC.

hoard

Collect and hide away large amounts of something.

horde

A crowd of people – often used by the tabloid press in a negative way.

REMEMBER

You might HOARD things in a cupbOARD. Being chased by angry HORDES of protesters would be an ORDEal.

EXAMPLE

"Drunken HORDES descended on the sleepy village."

holey

Full of holes.

holy

Sacred or associated with God.

wholly

Entirely or completely. Think whole.

EXAMPLE

"Sponges and Swiss cheese are WHOLLY HOLEY.

The Bible and Qur'an are WHOLLY HOLY."

---

houmous

A chickpea paste or dip.

humus

Organic matter in soil.

hummus

An alternative spelling of HOUMOUS.

EXAMPLE

"Wouldn't it be humorous if we put HUMUS
in their HOUMOUS?!"

humerus

The bone between your shoulder and elbow.

humorous

Funny.

REMEMBER

Fun fact: people sometimes refer to the HUMERUS
as the funny bone, but the funny bone isn't a bone at
all – it's actually a nerve (the ulnar nerve to be precise).

EXAMPLE

"Breaking my HUMERUS wasn't HUMOROUS! Oww!"

imply

Hint at something. Relates to **giving** information.

infer

Make an educated guess. Relates to **taking** information.

REMEMBER

The **speaker** does the IMPLYING.

The **listener** does the INFERRING.

EXAMPLE

"I INFER from your tone that you're IMPLYING they lied!"

incinerate

The process of destroying something in a fire.

insinuate

Sneakily suggest that something bad is true.

REMEMBER

Toxic waste is burned in an INCINERATOR. The process of burning produces CINders. INSINUATE contains SIN.

EXAMPLE

"Are you INSINUATING they had an affair?"

indolent

Lazy.

insolent

Rude.

REMEMBER

The INS of both INSOLENT and INSult.

EXAMPLE

"We will not tolerate INDOLENT or INSOLENT behaviour at this school."

---

insidious

Having a gradual but harmful effect.

invidious

Unjust or unfair. Likely to cause resentment or anger.

REMEMBER

Think of the SID in INSIDIOUS and SIDe effects,
and the VID in INVIDIOUS and liVID.

EXAMPLE

"The INSIDIOUS harassment within the workplace
has put the staff in an INVIDIOUS position."

inspirational

Intended to inspire.

inspiring

Creating encouragement, excitement or exhilaration.

REMEMBER

These words are often used interchangeably.

Something INSPIRING might put a SPRING in your step.

EXAMPLE

"She's a truly INSPIRATIONAL speaker.

Her talk on the history of art was INSPIRING!"

intense

Strong, extreme or forceful. Often describes feelings.

intensive

Thorough or vigorous. Often used with **course**.

intent

Determined.

EXAMPLE

"She was INTENT on finishing her INTENSIVE course of medicine, but the side effects were INTENSE."

---

its

Belonging to it.

it's

A contraction of **it is** or **it has**.

REMEMBER

If you can replace the word with **it is** or **it has**,
always write IT'S. Otherwise, write ITS.

EXAMPLE

"My dog loves chasing ITS tail.
IT'S one of his favourite things to do."

just deserts

When you get what you deserve.

just desserts

What, no main course?!

REMEMBER

Think of the SS as a double helping of DESSERT,

while both DESERTS and DEServe have just one S.

JUST DESSERTS sounds like my kind of restaurant...

kinaesthetic

Relates to awareness of the position and movement of body parts. Often refers to KINAESTHETIC – or tactile – learning, where you learn by touching and doing.

kinetic

Relates to movement.

REMEMBER

Think back to science lessons, where KINETIC energy was built up by movement.

knead

Work dough or clay with your hands.

kneed

Hit someone with a knee.

need

Require something. More than want.

REMEMBER

You KNEAD the dough that becomes brEAD. Both share the same ending. And, of course, KNEED contains KNEE.

knight

A chess piece, medieval warrior, or rank awarded

by royalty in recognition of outstanding work.

night

The opposite of day.

REMEMBER

Conveniently, KNIGHTED is almost a perfect anagram

of THE KING – one of the few people with the ability

to KNIGHT someone.

lead (noun)

A heavy metal, or something you attach to a dog's collar.

lead (verb)

Guide, be in command of, or be in a winning position.

led

The past tense of LEAD.

REMEMBER

Be vigilant! LED and LEAD (noun) sound the same, meaning the past tense of LEAD is often mistakenly spelled LEAD.

lead a stray

Guide a homeless dog.

lead astray

Cause someone to behave badly.

lead ashtray

Potential weapon in Cluedo?!

REMEMBER

While the other two technically make sense,
LEAD ASTRAY is the commonly used phrase.

---

leant

The past tense of lean.

lent

The past tense of lend, or the period preceding Easter.

REMEMBER

LEAN becomes LEANT, LEND becomes LENT.

EXAMPLE

"I've LEANT on him for support for years.

He's LENT me money more than once."

---

lessen

Reduce.

lesson

Learning session.

REMEMBER

To create a LESSER amount of something,
you LESSEN the quantity.

EXAMPLE

"Since our curriculum was LESSENED,
our LESSONS have been much shorter."

lets (noun)

Rented properties.

lets (verb)

Allows.

let's

Contraction of **let us**.

EXAMPLE

"This key LETS you unlock the door to our summer holiday LET. LET'S go!"

---

liable

Legally responsible for, or susceptible to.

libel

A published false – often malicious – statement
that could damage someone's reputation.

REMEMBER

LIBEL is written: written materials are kept in a LIBrary.

EXAMPLE

"After she lost her LIBEL claim in court, she was LIABLE
to pay legal fees."

libellous

Relating to libel: defamation in **writing**.

slanderous

Relating to slander: defamation in **speech**.

REMEMBER

A LIBELLOUS statement is **written** (think LIBrary).

A SLANDEROUS statement is **spoken** (both start with S).

EXAMPLE

"At first it was just SLANDEROUS. Then the newspapers printed the speech! Now it's LIBELLOUS."

---

licence (noun)

A document that allows someone to do something.

license (verb)

The act of officially allowing someone to do something.

REMEMBER

Much like ADVICE and ADVISE, DEVICE and DEVISE, PRACTICE and PRACTISE, the C spelling is the noun.

EXAMPLE

"You know you need a LICENCE to drive
– and I can't LICENSE you until you pass your test."

lightening

Making something lighter in weight or colour.

lightning

A flash in the sky, accompanied by thunder. Often used as an adjective to describe something incredibly fast.

REMEMBER

To LIGHTEN something is to make it LIGHTer, hence the spelling of LIGHTENING.

EXAMPLE

"LIGHTNING does a good job of LIGHTENING the sky."

---

literal

Exactly as stated.

littoral

The area between high and low tide points on a shore.

REMEMBER

LITERAL means taking words exactly as written,
so think of LITERAture, which is full of words.

EXAMPLE

"Not many people know the LITERAL meaning
of the word LITTORAL."

---

loath

Unwilling or reluctant.

loathe

Despise.

REMEMBER

Somewhat appropriately, the ATHE of LOATHE

is an anagram of HATE.

EXAMPLE

"I'm LOATH to admit that I LOATHE slugs.

What's the point of them?!"

loose

Wobbly, or not firmly fixed.

lose

Misplace something.

REMEMBER

Blame the pronunciation for the confusion here. LOSE
looks like it should be pronounced LOZE (like rOSE or hOSE),
but is pronounced LOOZE. LOOSE rhymes with gOOSE,
so picture a gOOSE with LOOSE feathers. The dafter
the picture, the more likely it'll stick in your mind.

loyalest

Most loyal.

loyalist

Someone fiercely loyal to a government or ruler.

REMEMBER

The suffix EST adds the word **most** to any adjective.

Just as **warm** becomes **warmest** and **big** becomes

biggest, LOYAL becomes LOYALEST.

EXAMPLE

"Who is the LOYALEST LOYALIST in town?"

---

m

manner

The attitude with which something is done.

manor

A large country house surrounded by land.

REMEMBER

Taunting "NER NER NE NER NERRRR" is bad MANNERS.

EXAMPLE

"He swaggered through the entrance hall of the MANOR in a pretentious MANNER. Anyone would've thought he'd owned the place!"

marinade (noun)

Sauce for marinating.

marinate (verb)

Soak food in a MARINADE to add flavour.

REMEMBER

Think of lemonADE to remember that MARINADE

is a liquid.

EXAMPLE

"Remember to MARINATE the chicken before you stick

it on the barbecue. I added chilli to the MARINADE."

---

mat

Something to wipe your feet on, or to lay the dinner table with.

matt

A non-shiny finish – or at least one person you know.

matte

The American English spelling of MATT.

EXAMPLE

"MATT spilled MATT paint on the new MAT!"

merengue

Caribbean dance.

meringue

Sugar-based dessert.

REMEMBER

Confuse these two and you'll end up with more than
an Eton mess! The word MERINGUE (pronounced
mer-ang) ends IN GUE. In fact, the recipe starts
IN GOO that's made from sugar and egg whites.

---

meter

A device for measuring, or the US spelling of METRE.

metre

A unit of measurement, equivalent to 100 centimetres.

REMEMBER

The measurement is spelled METRE in British English and METER in American English. Endings are the same for the British English spelling of cenTRE and the US cenTER. You feed a parking METER with coins, while a parking METRE... an insanely small parking space?!

momentary

Brief.

momentous

Very significant – such as a historic event.

REMEMBER

The suffix OUS means **full of**. Think of MOMENTOUS
as being a MOMENT full of significance.

EXAMPLE

"That MOMENTARY lapse in judgement led
to the team's most MOMENTOUS defeat."

---

moorish

Relating to the Moors and their culture.

moreish

Something so yummy you want more of it. Cake, anyone?

REMEMBER

When you want MORE of something, it's MOREISH.

EXAMPLE

"That traditional MOORISH orange cake is so MOREISH.
I could eat it all day!"

moot point

Refers to something that's subject to uncertainty or debate – and, more recently, an issue that's irrelevant because it's practically impossible to answer. It's not...

mute point

REMEMBER

A common mistake is thinking the phrase refers to a closed matter – something that's MUTE. Remember the episode of Friends when Joey and Rachel discussed the expression? Nope – it's not a MOO POINT either.

muscles

Built up through exercise.

mussels

Edible squirmy creatures.

REMEMBER

Think of the SSE in MUSSELS, which are found in the Salty SEa.

EXAMPLE

"MUSSELS contain protein, which is good for building up your MUSCLES."

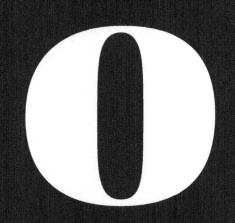

oar

Wooden paddle used to propel a boat or raft.

or

Used to link alternatives.

ore

Material from which metal or minerals can be extracted.

EXAMPLE

"Use the OARS to steer the boat to the cave. We'll mine for ORE and sell the minerals OR metal we extract."

---

objective

Factual or non-biased.

subjective

Based on personal preference or opinion.

REMEMBER

An OBJECT looks the same to everyone, while most SUBJECTs generate a range of opinions.

EXAMPLE

"Art is SUBJECTIVE – but the parking at this gallery is OBJECTIVELY bad!"

The phrase...

old wives' tale

is a traditional belief based on superstition. Not...

old wise tale

REMEMBER

An OLD WIVES' TALE is generally considered to be untrue. Calling it an OLD WISE TALE implies sayings such as 'If you don't eat your crusts your hair won't curl!' are based on wisdom. (And no, it's not an OLD WIVES' TAIL or an OLD WISE TAIL either!)

The phrase...

off your own bat

means independently or using your initiative. Not...

off your own back

REMEMBER

OFF YOUR OWN BACK is a mishearing of the phrase
OFF YOUR OWN BAT, which has its origins in cricket.

EXAMPLE

"I swear it was nothing to do with me!
They did it OFF THEIR OWN BAT."

---

omelette

A simple supper made from eggs.

umlaut

Two dots over a vowel – commonly used in German
– to change pronunciation. Yüm.

REMEMBER

Just as the word OMELETTE contains three Es,
the best OMELETTES contain three Eggs. Or call it
an OM-EE-LETT-EE. That works, too. (Where's the
grinning face emoji when you need it?!)

---

ordinance

A law or authoritative rule.

ordnance

Military supplies, such as weapons and ammunition.

REMEMBER

The only difference in the spelling of these two words is the I in ORDINANCE. To remember the difference, think of how laws involve dotting 'i's and crossing 't's. The British national mapping agency has its roots in military strategy, hence its name, ORDNANCE Survey.

The sensation of floating outside your own body is an...

out-of-body

experience, not an...

outer body

experience.

REMEMBER

Think of OUT as a shortening of OUTSIDE to remember
that an OUT-OF-BODY experience is the feeling of
being OUTSIDE your own body – or disconnected
from events going on around you.

pacific

Large ocean.

specific

Precise.

REMEMBER

To remember SPECIFIC, think of SPECIFICation

– a precise description.

EXAMPLE

"Are you referring to the Atlantic Ocean or the PACIFIC?

You must be more SPECIFIC."

---

pair

A group of two things, or the act of grouping two things.

pare

Trim, or reduce in size.

pear

A juicy green fruit.

EXAMPLE

"If I PARE down this PAIR of PEARS, I'll have one left."

paltry

Trivial, or a laughably small amount.

poultry

Domestic fowl, or meat from chickens,

turkeys, geese and ducks.

REMEMBER

PALTRY contains the A of Amount.

EXAMPLE

"The restaurant is largely plant-based.

There's a PALTRY amount of POULTRY on the menu."

---

parameter

A boundary or limit that affects how something functions.

perimeter

The boundary of an area or object.

REMEMBER

Both words have their roots in science and mathematics but can also be used more generally. A debate can have PARAMETERS, as can a brief. Your garden might have a PERIMETER fence, while the police might set a PERIMETER to secure the scene of a crime.

passed

Past tense of pass, meaning moved by, gave to, opted out of, elapsed or didn't fail. Got that?!

past

Any time before the present or, in writing, a tense used to describe PAST events. Also, further than or beyond.

REMEMBER

PASS is a verb, so PASSED relates to action.

EXAMPLE

"The time for thinking about the PAST has PASSED."

patience

Tolerance.

patients

People receiving medical treatment.

REMEMBER

PATIENCE and toleraNCE both end in NCE. PATIENTS may be treated by an ENT (ear, nose and throat) specialist.

EXAMPLE

"Even after a 12-hour shift you mustn't lose PATIENCE with your PATIENTS."

---

peace

Quiet, calmness, or the opposite of war.

piece

Fragment, or a share of something, such as pizza.

REMEMBER

Think PIECE of PIzza – both start with PI.

EXAMPLE

"If he doesn't stop banging on about insurance providing PEACE of mind I'll give him a PIECE of my mind!"

---

peak

The top of a mountain, the brim of a cap, or the height of something, such as achievement.

peek

Take a quick look.

pique

Arouse curiosity, or anger someone.

EXAMPLE

"I PIQUED his interest with a sneak PEEK of the PEAK."

---

perspective

Point of view, or attitude towards something.

prospective

Probable or expected. Relates to the future.

REMEMBER

A business you want to work with in future is a
PROSPECTIVE client. A PERSPECTIVE client is not a thing.

EXAMPLE

"From my PERSPECTIVE, these PROSPECTIVE buyers
have made the best offer we're going to get."

poisonous

If you bite it and you die, it's POISONOUS.

venomous

If it bites you and you die, it's VENOMOUS.

REMEMBER

POISON is **ingested**. VENOM is **injected**. To remember the difference, think of the V in Viper – a VENOMOUS snake.

EXAMPLE

"He'd survived being bitten by a VENOMOUS snake. I guess he didn't know the mushrooms were POISONOUS!"

practice (noun)

The act of practising, the application of theory,

or a doctor or lawyer's place of work.

practise (verb)

Repeat something regularly with the aim of improving.

REMEMBER

Think of the rule: ICE = noun. 'Best PRACTICE' is a noun.

EXAMPLE

"You should PRACTISE kung fu regularly.

Mastery comes with PRACTICE."

precede

Come before.

proceed

Go ahead, or continue.

REMEMBER

The prefix PRE means **before**.

EXAMPLE

"Everyone please PROCEED to the main hall – the headteacher's speech will PRECEDE registration."

precedence

Priority. Often used with **take**.

precedents

Past experiences, used as examples for the future.

presidents

Leaders of an organisation or country.

REMEMBER

Think of the PRECEDE in PRECEDENCE to remember it comes before in importance. PRESIDENT is always a noun.

preceding

Coming before.

proceeding

Going ahead, continuing, or a legal action.

REMEMBER

The prefix PRE means **before**.

EXAMPLE

"The legal team already decided they're PROCEEDING with court PROCEEDINGS. They discussed plans in the PRECEDING meeting."

price

Cost. Something given in exchange for something else.

prise

Force open, or get something with difficulty.

prize

An award.

REMEMBER

To PRISE the lid off a jar of jam is to encourage
it to RISE.

principal

Main, or most important. Also the head of a school, college, or organisation.

principle

A fundamental truth or belief.

REMEMBER

My PAL the PRINCIPAL.

EXAMPLE

"My PRINCIPAL goal is to become PALs with the PRINCIPAL. His educational PRINCIPLES are sound."

prodigy

Someone who demonstrates extreme talent or aptitude.
Often used with **child**.

progeny

Offspring. A descendant of a person, plant or animal.

REMEMBER

Think of the GEN in PROGENY to remember the
connection with future GENerations.

EXAMPLE

"My PROGENY is a piano PRODIGY."

program

Computer code, or the act of writing computer code.

programme

An itinerary or set of events, or a TV show.

REMEMBER

British English typically uses PROGRAM for anything
computer-related, and PROGRAMME for everything else.
American English uses PROGRAM for both meanings.

EXAMPLE

"The PROGRAMME includes time learning to PROGRAM."

---

prostate

A gland near the bladder in males (human and animal).

prostrate

Face down on the ground.

REMEMBER

The word PROSTATE is all too often associated with cancer – which is why it's important for a doctor to check it's in a healthy STATE. Someone lying PROSTRATE could be super Relaxed (remember the R).

rack (noun)

A type of storage – often for clothing or footwear – or a means of displaying items.

rack (verb)

Torture, or cause to suffer. While the expressions 'RACK your brain', 'RACK and ruin' and 'RACKED with guilt' are more commonly spelled RACK, they can also be spelled...

wrack

Relates to wreckage or destruction. Now commonly used as a variant spelling of RACK (verb).

rap

Form of music mastered by Snoop Dogg, Jay-Z and the like. Also a sharp blow, or the act of knocking.

wrap

Envelop, an item used for wrapping, or a soft tortilla.

REMEMBER

You 'WRAP things up' when you finish a project (hence 'That's a WRAP!' in the movie industry). The phrase is 'get a bad RAP', not 'get a bad WRAP'. (If you get a bad WRAP you might want to complain to the chef.)

reconcile

Resolve, or restore.

rectify

Fix, or make right.

REMEMBER

Remember the F in RECTIFY and Fix, and the connection between RECONCILE and RECONCILIATION. You might 'RECONCILE your differences' to make peace with an ex-friend – and let's hope you RECTIFY the mistakes in your email before hitting send!

---

recur

Happen regularly or repeatedly.

reoccur

Happen again.

REMEMBER

Handily, the word REOCCUR contains OCCUR to remind you it's the word to use when something OCCURS once again. It might help to remember that a RECURRING decimal goes on infinitely. (While a REOCCURRING decimal would OCCUR at least Once again.)

---

regime

A form of government. Sometimes used to mean...

regimen

A systematic plan to improve your health or fitness,

often involving diet, medication or exercise.

REMEMBER

REGIMEN and plaN both end in N.

EXAMPLE

"I spend ages on my skincare REGIMEN each night."

regimental

Relating to a regiment.

regimented

Carefully organised, or strictly controlled.

REMEMBER

REGIMENTED, organisED and controllED all end in ED.

EXAMPLE

"REGIMENTAL guidelines require a REGIMENTED approach to personal appearance. And a damn short haircut!"

---

reign

A monarch's rule.

rein

A long strap used to control a horse, or a guiding power.

REMEMBER

REIGN can be a noun or a verb, but always relates to leadership or control – usually over a country and sometimes over a situation. Chaos REIGNS (not REINS), you 'REIN it in' and the phrase related to freedom of action or expression is spelled 'free REIN' (not free REIGN).

---

retch

Gag, or make the action of vomiting.

wretch

An unfortunate or deeply unhappy person. Someone you might feel sorry for.

REMEMBER

RETCHED (pronounced rech-d) is the past tense of RETCH. WRETCHED (pronounced rech-ed) might be used to describe deep feelings of unhappiness – but it can also mean someone morally reprehensible.

---

right

Correct, the opposite of left, or a moral entitlement
(such as human rights).

rite

A ritual or ceremony – often religious.

write

Put words on paper.

EXAMPLE

"WRITE about the RITE the RIGHT way."

---

rind

The entire covering of a citrus fruit.

zest

The fine outer part of a citrus fruit.

(Who else thought they were the same thing?!)

REMEMBER

ZEST can also mean great enthusiasm, or joie de vivre.

EXAMPLE

"She has an incredible ZEST for life!"

---

role

A job, function, or part played.

roll

A form of baked dough, or to move by rotation.

REMEMBER

A job is always a ROLE, not a ROLL. (Unless you're
dressed up advertising a fast food restaurant, I guess...)
Truly, you're not delighted to have played 'an important
ROLL in the project'.

S

sail

Travel by boat.

sale

Goods going cheap.

REMEMBER

To go anywhere in a SAILboat, you have to raise the SAILS.

You might 'SAIL through' something easy.

EXAMPLE

"There's a SALE on SAILING gear down at the marina."

---

scald

Burn with hot liquid.

scold

Tell off.

REMEMBER

If you SCOLD someone too often, they might think of you as being COLD.

EXAMPLE

"You might SCOLD yourself if you SCALD yourself."

Someone used to avoid consequences is called a...

scapegoat

Not an...

escape goat

REMEMBER

A SCAPEGOAT used to refer to the goat that was
sacrificed to absolve the sins of other people.
Now it refers to a way to escape the consequences
of something – so it's retained some of its meaning.

scents

Smells.

sense

Logic or feeling.

50 cent

American rapper.

50 cents

Half a dollar.

sever

Cut off.

severe

Serious or intense in a negative way.

REMEMBER

SEVER has no E. You could say the ending of the word has been cut off. (Okay, so it was never there in the first place. Semantics!)

EXAMPLE

"A SEVERED arm is considered a SEVERE wound."

---

should of

This is a mishearing of...

should've

A contraction of **should have**.

REMEMBER

Think of the VE of haVE and SHOULD'VE.

Never write SHOULD OF – it's always wrong.

The same goes for COULD OF and WOULD OF.

EXAMPLE

"You SHOULD'VE told me it was your birthday!"

simulate

Imitate something.

stimulate

Revive or encourage.

REMEMBER

Think of the popular SIMs video game, which is designed to be a SIMULATION of real life.

EXAMPLE

"Trainee pilots use flight SIMULATORS to train – and to STIMULATE their desire to fly."

---

sleight

A deceptive move.

slight

Small. Also an insult.

REMEMBER

If you're trying to become Smaller and LIGHTer
(S + LIGHT), you eat SLIGHTLY less than normal.

EXAMPLE

"They say a magician never reveals his secrets, but
I caught a SLIGHT glimpse of his SLEIGHT of hand."

---

slither

Move in a snake-like way.

sliver

A thin slice.

REMEMBER

SLITHER for snake, SLIVER for cake. The symbol of Slytherin house in the Harry Potter novels is a snake.

EXAMPLE

"I was enjoying a SLIVER of cake when I saw a snake SLITHER through the grass. It made me shiver!"

sort

Variety or type, or the action of putting things into categories, or order.

sought

Searched for. Past tense of seek.

REMEMBER

The OR in ORder and SORT.

EXAMPLE

"He only SOUGHT to SORT out my stationery drawer, but ended up reorganising my whole office!"

---

spacious

Roomy.

specious

Misleading or deceitful.

REMEMBER

Somewhere SPACIOUS has plenty of SPACe.

EXAMPLE

"The ad said the apartment was SPACIOUS.
Having seen it, the statement was more
SPECIOUS than true."

spare

Excess, or one step down from a strike in bowling.

spur

Incentivise or encourage, or a cowboy boot appendage.

REMEMBER

Something that keeps you motivated to succeed
'SPURS you on'. The phrase meaning impulsive,
or without planning, is 'SPUR of the moment'.
'SPARE of the moment' isn't a thing (other than,
arguably, a winning shot in a game of ten-pin bowling...).

stationary

Not moving.

stationery

Paper and pens.

REMEMBER

The AR in pARked cAR and STATIONARY.

The ER in papER and STATIONERY. Or E for Envelope.

EXAMPLE

You sit in STATIONARY traffic, not STATIONERY traffic (unless it's a queue of Office World vans).

---

straight

Free from curves. Also, heterosexual.

strait

A narrow, connecting stream of water. When used with **dire**, STRAITS also refers to a difficult situation.

REMEMBER

Someone emotionless can be described as 'STRAIGHT-faced', while 'STRAIT-laced' – which describes someone with strict morals – can also be spelled 'STRAIGHT-laced'. The correct moral path is 'the STRAIGHT and narrow'.

---

suit

A formal outfit, usually involving a jacket and trousers.

suite

A room in a hotel, or a set of musical compositions.

sweet

A dessert or a candy. Also cute or kind.

REMEMBER

You wear a three-piece SUIT. You sit on a three-piece SUITE
(a sofa and two chairs). You eat a three-piece SWEET.

---

summary

A synopsis of key points.

summery

Having the characteristics of summer.

REMEMBER

You say 'to SUMMARISE...' before providing a short SUMMARY of key points.

EXAMPLE

"In SUMMARY, my outfit was especially SUMMERY."

suppose

Presume.

supposed

Presumed.

REMEMBER

Keep the ED at the end of SUPPOSED and presumED
in mind to remember that SUPPOSED is past tense.

EXAMPLE

"I SUPPOSE that was SUPPOSED to happen."
(Not SUPPOSE to happen.)

tack

A round-headed pin.

tact

The ability to handle a difficult or awkward situation without causing offence or hurting anyone's feelings.

REMEMBER

TACT requires you to ACT with sensitivity. Taking a fresh approach to something is called 'changing TACK' – a nautical term for a change of direction. A clever person might be described as being 'sharp as a TACK'.

---

tail

The part of the dog that wags, or the end
of a process or thing, such as a plane.

tale

A story.

REMEMBER

A 'tall TALE' is a fantastical, hard-to-believe story.
Only a giraffe has a tall TAIL.

EXAMPLE

"Remember the TALE about the monkey that lost its TAIL?"

---

taxes

Amounts paid to the government based on your income or the cost of goods or services you're buying.

taxis

More than one taxi.

REMEMBER

We would all be wealthier if TAXES were AXEd.

EXAMPLE

"Let's face it – most of us can't afford to travel in TAXIS once we've paid our TAXES!"

---

tenant

Inhabitant of a rented property.

tenet

A central belief or principle.

REMEMBER

TENANT and inhabitANT both end in ANT.

EXAMPLE

"One of my core TENETS is giving my TENANTS back their full deposit." (Said no landlord, ever.)

tentative

Provisional, hesitant or uncertain.

tenuous

Weak, insubstantial or dubious.

REMEMBER

TENUOUS and dubiOUS have the same ending. You might make TENTATIVE plans after a TENUOUS argument.

EXAMPLE

"Proceed TENTATIVELY with your investigation: the connection between suspects is TENUOUS, at best."

When you feel a sense of worried anticipation, you're on...

tenterhooks

Not...

tender hooks

(Which sound like something a kindly pirate might use.)

REMEMBER

The phrase is based on the word TENTER, which was a frame used to dry and stretch cloth. The TENTERHOOK kept the cloth tense and tight – hence the expression. A TENDER HOOK is not a thing.

---

their

Belonging to them.

there

Refers to location (both literal and figurative).

they're

A contraction of **they are**.

REMEMBER

Hello THERE! Get clear on the meaning of THEIR and THEY'RE, and use THERE for everything else.

---

there'll

A contraction of **there will** or **there shall**.

they'll

A contraction of **they will** or **they shall**.

REMEMBER

As long as you know if you're referring to THERE or THEY, you can't go wrong.

EXAMPLE

"THERE'LL be trouble if you mix these up. Those grammar police – THEY'LL be after you!"

to

Shows motion, or the infinitive form of a verb: TO be.

too

Also, or excessively.

two

Number between one and three.

REMEMBER

TO has TOO many meanings to list! Learn the meaning
of TOO and TWO, and use TO for everything else.

---

toe

Five make a foot.

tow

Lead or pull.

REMEMBER

You 'TOE the line' when you conform. 'TOW the line' is wrong (unless you're taking part in a tug of war, perhaps).

EXAMPLE

"Would you TOW my car home? I don't think I can drive with this broken TOE!"

tortoise

Slow-moving reptile.

tortuous

Winding and crooked, or lengthy and complex.

torturous

Causing pain or suffering.

totoro

Lovable character from an animé movie.

u

uncharted

Unexplored or unmapped.

unchartered

Having no charter.

REMEMBER

UNCHARTED is by far the more common of the two words and can be used in a figurative sense – to describe unfamiliar situations – not just a literal, geographic one. The phrase 'UNCHARTED territory' is often misspelled as 'UNCHARTERED territory', so watch out for this one.

---

unkempt

Messy or dishevelled. Often used with **hair**.

unkept

Neglected and uncared for. Also relates to broken commitments or promises.

REMEMBER

Both UNKEMPT and UNKEPT can relate to appearance, but UNKEMPT (think uncombed) is commonly used to describe people, while UNKEPT is more often used to describe places.

use to

Use something for a particular purpose.

used to

In the habit of doing. Or something that happened in the past but no longer happens.

REMEMBER

You might write 'I'm USED TO juggling work and family commitments' (aren't we all), or 'I USED TO dance regularly, but rarely have time these days'. Just don't write 'I USE TO dance regularly'.

V

vain

Conceited.

vane

Device that indicates wind direction. Used with **weather**.

vein

A blood vessel. Used with **in the same** to imply likeness.

REMEMBER

Something done 'in VAIN' is a fruitless task. Something done 'in VEIN' is intravenous. Don't mix those two up.

---

verses

More than one verse.

versus

Against. Often abbreviated to **v** or **vs**.

REMEMBER

To remember the spelling of VERSUS, think about how team sport is 'them against US'.

EXAMPLE

"She sung the first two VERSES of the national anthem at the England VERSUS Australia match."

viola

Stringed instrument, or a small pansy-like flower.

voilà

An exclamation – much like ta-da – pronounced vwa-lah.

REMEMBER

Think about the accent on the final A of VOILÀ to remember that VOILÀ is used as an exclamation.

EXAMPLE

"VOILÀ! Behold my new VIOLA!"

waist

The area above your hips.

waste

Unwanted materials, or to expend carelessly.

REMEMBER

Think of the spelling of WASTEful to remember WASTE.
WAISTful isn't a word.

EXAMPLE

"You WASTE too much time worrying about the size
of your WAIST. Just enjoy the meal!"

---

wander

Move aimlessly.

wonder

Be curious. Or something exceptional.

REMEMBER

WONDER is synonymous with pONDER, which shares the same ending. WANDER contains the A of Aimless.

EXAMPLE

"I'd love to WANDER around the Seven WONDERS of the World. I WONDER when they were built?"

warrior

An adept fighter or enduring person.

worrier

An adept stresser or anxious person.

wario

Mario's arch enemy and the owner of one of the best fictional moustaches.

REMEMBER

Think of the WAR in WARRIOR and WORRY for WORRIER.

---

way

A method, or the path taken to get somewhere.

weigh

Assess – usually in relation to how heavy something is.

whey

The liquid that separates from curdled milk.

EXAMPLE

"As an experienced cheesemaker, you'll be familiar
with the correct WAY to WEIGH the WHEY."

---

weak

Lacking in strength – physically or mentally.

week

A period of time lasting seven days
(usually from Monday to Sunday).

REMEMBER

A cup of tEA can be WEAK. Both words share EA.

EXAMPLE

"Not sure I'll make the end-of-WEEK meeting.
I've been feeling pretty WEAK all day."

---

wear

What you do with clothes, or damage as a result of use.

where

Relating to a place or situation.

REMEMBER

Think of the expression 'WEAR and tEAR'. Both words end in EAR. WHERE contains HERE – a possible answer to the question.

EXAMPLE

"WHERE do you WEAR those fancy clothes?"

weather

The state of the atmosphere, if you want to get technical. Sun and rain, if you don't. To 'WEATHER the storm' is to successfully handle a difficult situation.

whether

Expresses choice or doubt between options.

EXAMPLE

"Today's WEATHER is unpredictable. I don't know WHETHER to bring my coat."

weir

A structure built in a river to divert the flow of water.

we're

A contraction of **we are**.

REMEMBER

If you can replace the word with **we are**, write WE'RE.

EXAMPLE

"WE'RE really enjoying the view of the WEIR
from our weird holiday cottage in Tyne and Wear!"

---

were

Past tense of are or be.

whir

A monotonous sound, usually associated with technology.

whirr

Alternative spelling of WHIR.

EXAMPLE

"The WHIRRS from the propeller WERE quite off-putting."

wet

The opposite of dry, or the process of wetting.

whet

Stimulate, or sharpen.

REMEMBER

You 'WET your whistle' when you quench your thirst, but might 'WHET your appetite' with a snack when you're hungry. The abrasive block used to sharpen a blade is called a WHETSTONE. (A WET stone isn't going to sharpen anything.)

The phrase meaning pale-faced, often due to shock is...

white as a sheet

Not...

white as a sheep

Sharing the same colour as a sheep's wool.

REMEMBER

Try to remember that not all sheep are white

(and forget that the same is true of bedsheets).

who's

A contraction of **who is** or **who has**.

whose

A possessive pronoun relating to whom.

REMEMBER

If you can replace the word with **who is** or **who has**,
write WHO'S.

EXAMPLE

"WHOSE stupid idea was that?!"
"I don't know! WHO'S got a better idea?"

would of

This is a mishearing of...

would've

A contraction of **would have**.

REMEMBER

Think of the VE of haVE and WOULD'VE.

Never write WOULD OF – it's always wrong.

The same goes for COULD OF and SHOULD OF.

EXAMPLE

"I WOULD'VE come to the party if I'd known about it!"

y

yore

Long, long ago. Usually used with **days of**.

your

Something that belongs to you.

you're

A contraction of **you are**.

REMEMBER

If you can replace the word with **you are**, write YOU'RE.

The word YORE is rarely used.

you'll

A contraction of **you will**.

yule

An archaic term for the Christmas period.

REMEMBER

If you can replace the word with **you will**, write YOU'LL.

Let's face it – you're pretty unlikely to need the word

YULE – unless you're writing about deliciously chocolatey

Christmas cakes (damn you, gluten intolerance!).

young

In the early stages of life. Opposite of old.

youthful

Characteristic of youth.

REMEMBER

YOUNG people are naturally YOUTHFUL, but you can be described as YOUTHFUL at any age. You could be known for your YOUTHFUL enthusiasm, YOUTHFUL energy or YOUTHFUL looks, long after you lost the right to be described as YOUNG (lucky you!).

CONCLUSION

I originally had the idea for **The Little Book of Confusables** back in 2017, when I knew absolutely nothing about publishing a book. I met with a local author at the time, to find out what I could. She shared her advice on the subject, and – unbeknown to her – completely terrified me in the process!

I wasn't ready – and neither was the idea.

Fast forward five years and I'm still spotting the same errors, day in, day out. Having gone through the steepest of learning curves from publishing **Survival Skills for Freelancers** in 2020, I decided it was time to revisit the idea.

This time, I was ready. I hope you love reading it as much as I loved writing it.

Undoubtedly the hardest part of writing this book was knowing where to draw the line – and the list of **confusables** I didn't have space to include is already growing! If you have a favourite that I haven't included, drop me an email. Who knows... maybe it'll appear in the sequel!

NEXT STEPS

If you've enjoyed this book, I have a favour to ask: please pop online and **leave a review** on Amazon. Each positive review helps me to help more readers just like you become confident writers.

- Stay in touch by joining my Clever Copy Club. Sign up at **sarahtownsendeditorial.co.uk/email-newsletter-signup/**

- Share the love and tag me on social media using **#confusables** for the chance to be shared or featured. (Bonus points if you include a pic!)

    Instagram @thecopywritersday

    Twitter @STEcopywriting

    LinkedIn Sarah Townsend Editorial

    Facebook Sarah Townsend Editorial

- Check out my bestselling guide to self-employment – **Survival Skills for Freelancers** – at **survivalskillsforfreelancers.com** or on Amazon, worldwide.

- Finally, help your **family**, **friends** and **colleagues** avoid the stupid mistakes even smart people make. How? By telling them about this book! Better still, why not buy them a copy?

I hope **The Little Book of Confusables** helps you supercharge your vocabulary, write with confidence, and avoid those embarrassing mistakes we all worry about making. Let me know how you get on!

Thanks for reading.

Sarah x

ACKNOWLEDGEMENTS

Huge thanks to **Andy Hussey** from Lost and Found Creative for my fabulous cover, design consultancy and layout, **Rich Bell** from Maple Rock for landing page and website design, **Rebecca Lowe** for proofreading, **Kate Levitt-Hellier** and **Millie Andrews** for admin assistance, **Vicky Plum** for my author photo and both **Jez Wallace** and **Amy Townsend** for emotional support (and regular reminders to eat!).

Above all, huge thanks to my son – and tireless sounding board (he may not agree with the tireless bit!) – **George Townsend**, who spent his last summer before university working with me on **The Little Book of Confusables**.

Chances are you wouldn't be reading this book had it not been for his creative input and ideas, as well as editorial, layout and admin support.

(You could even say the book's existence was **DEPENDENT** on my **DEPENDANT**. Sorry!)

Printed in Great Britain
by Amazon

86461606R00190